P9-DEZ-941

Amelia Earhart

Amelia Earhart

Academic Industries, Inc.
West Haven, Connecticut 06516

ISBN 0-88301-773-3

Published by
Academic Industries, Inc.
The Academic Building
Saw Mill Road
West Haven, Connecticut 06516

Printed in the United States of America

Amelia Earhart

Contents

She was a brave woman who had the will to prove that women could equal men—in flying and in life itself.

She was Amelia Earhart, the first woman to fly over the Atlantic Ocean in an airplane. First she flew as a passenger, then alone in her own small, single-engine airplane.

Looks like there's a storm coming.

Yes, they have bad storms here.

Amelia Earhart was born in Atchison, Kansas, on July 24, 1898. Her grandparents had arrived years before in a covered wagon.

9

The Adventurous Young Girl

In her grandmother's time there were still many Indians in Kansas.

Don't worry, they're friendly.

I know . . . but they scare me!

Amelia traveled in a very different way.

I wish I'd been a pioneer like Grandma, with Indians and covered wagons.

There are always pioneers, Amelia . . . and new worlds to discover!

Amelia's father was a lawyer for the railroad. He traveled a great deal. She and her sister Muriel spent a lot of time with their grandparents in Atchison.

Next stop . . . Atchison.

I can hardly wait!

13

The girls loved Grandma and Grandpa Otis. But sometimes there were problems.

Girls! What are you wearing this morning?

Bloomers, Grandma! Mother sent them!

They're much better than skirts. We can run and play in them.

But girls don't wear such things!

Now go upstairs and put on your dresses!

Yes, Grandma.

Once, as a special treat, their father took the girls to the St. Louis World's Fair.

I'm flying! It's wonderful!

Back in Atchison again, Amelia had an idea.

Let's build a roller coaster!

But—how can we?

We'll make a track by nailing these boards to the roof!

For a car I can put my roller skates on the bottom of this box.

We'll draw straws to see who goes first.

Oh, you go, Amelia.

You worked hardest!

POCKET BIOGRAPHIES

A happy Amelia climbed to the top of the slide. She sat down and gave a push.

Here I come! It's great!

At the end of the track the car hit the ground and stopped. Amelia flew through the air!

Ooooooh!

Are you hurt, Amelia?

Of course not! I see what's wrong. The track must come out farther at the bottom. Let's fix it!

But Grandma put a stop to their plans.

That thing is dangerous! Why did you do such a thing, Amelia?

For fun, Grandma!

Amelia's
First Flights

Amelia enjoyed reading adventure stories.

Reading is a nice way for a young lady to spend her time.

Why shouldn't girls have adventures? Someday I will!

One thing makes me mad, though. The heroes are always boys or men!

In 1908, when Amelia was ten years old, her father took the girls to the Iowa State Fair.

Please, Papa . . . one more ride?

I want to ride the *real* ponies!

Let's go to see the flying machine instead!

At last they reached the flying field.

The first aeroplane flew only five years ago. Now you are seeing one!

But Amelia didn't think much of the airplane.

Several years passed. Muriel went to college in Toronto, Canada. In 1917, during World War I, Amelia went to visit her.

Oh, Muriel, until I came here I never knew what war meant!

It's not just soldiers and bands playing. It's men being hurt! I must stay and help!

The hospitals are full of wounded men.

Amelia wrote to her mother.

Instead of returning to school, I want to become a nurses' aide.

Her mother agreed to let her stay.

She worked at the Spadina Military Hospital for twelve hours every day.

She scrubbed floors.

She helped the wounded men.

Would you rub my back?

She carried trays.

Not rice pudding *again!*

For the rest of her life, Amelia would be strongly against war.

Once, when she was not working, a friend took Amelia to the airfield where the Royal Air Corps was trained.

So that's what flying can be! It's so beautiful!!

Oh, Captain Spaulding, I want to fly!

I am really sorry, but there are rules against it.

I'm sorry, too. Someday I *will* fly!

When the war was over, Amelia went to New York and entered Columbia University. She would study to be a doctor. After a year she decided to leave school.

I'm sorry you are leaving. You would be a good doctor.

I just don't think this is my true work.

Amelia went to California. Her parents had moved there, and they wanted her to come and stay with them.

21

Soon after she arrived, her father took her to an air show. A surprised crowd watched as a man stood on the wing of a plane.

Another plane flew by. The man reached for a rope hanging from it, missed, reached again, and grabbed it.

He pulled himself to safety on the other plane. The crowd cheered.

Amelia watched happily as planes looped, dived, and spun in the air.

Oh, Papa! How much does it cost to learn to fly?

About a thousand dollars.

A thousand dollars! May I at least go up for a ride?

If you are brave enough. I'll see to it.

The pilot for her first flight was Frank Hawks, winner of many speed records.

It's the best thing in the world!

Now she knew she had to fly. To pay for lessons she found a job with the telephone company.

Oh! Time to go to work!

Weekends were for flying. Amelia's teacher was Neta Snook, the first woman to finish at the Curtiss School of Aviation.

Before you leave the ground, you must learn the parts of your plane.

23

Slowly Amelia learned to fly, sometimes the hard way. Once her plane flipped over on landing.

This looked like such a good, flat field!

There can always be a ditch that you can't see.

Later, Amelia took more lessons from John Montijo. He had taught Army pilots to fly.

I'm putting the plane into a spin. Take over and pull us out, Amelia!

Stunts are not just showing off, Amelia. They teach a pilot what to do when she's in trouble.

Okay.

At last the great day came when she could fly alone. She took her plane down the field and into the air.

She seems very calm.

She's a good pilot. To her, the plane is like part of herself!

For her twenty-fourth birthday, on July 24, 1922, Amelia's parents and Muriel helped her buy a small yellow plane.

It's exactly what I wanted—light enough so I can pick up the tail and turn it around myself!

That October, she gave her parents tickets to an air show at Rogers Field.

Ladies and gentlemen, Miss Amelia Earhart is about to try for a new women's altitude record!

That's my sister!

Amelia flew up and away until her little plane was only a speck in the sky.

She'll never make it in that small plane!

Later, she landed safely as the crowd cheered.

The sealed barograph from Miss Earhart's plane shows she reached 14,000 feet—a new women's record!

This was the first of many records Amelia would set.

A short time later, her parents decided to end their marriage.

Mother wants to go back to Boston with us. How will we do it?

There's only one way. I'll have to sell my plane.

With the money she received, Amelia bought a car.

EAST

Driving across the country is an adventure, too.

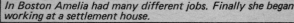
In Boston Amelia had many different jobs. Finally she began working at a settlement house.

I want to see how high I can pile them before they fall!

You are trying to learn something, Ferris. That's good!

Across
the Atlantic

One day in April, 1928, she and the children were preparing a play.

Telephone call for Miss Earhart!

Tell them to call back later. I'm busy.

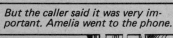

But the caller said it was very important. Amelia went to the phone.

This is Captain Hilton Railey. Will you do something important to help aviation?

I want you to fly across the Atlantic Ocean.

Of course! Who could turn down such an adventure?

What do you want me to do?

Mrs. Frederick Guest, an American, wanted a woman to make the flight. Captain Railey explained this to Amelia when she met him.

The year before, young Charles Lindbergh had flown the Atlantic Ocean alone to become a world hero. Three women had died trying to do the same.

Mrs. Guest has bought an airplane. She wants it to fly from America to England with a woman on board.

Would I be the pilot?

No. There will be a male pilot and a mechanic.

I see.

If you are interested, you must go to New York. There they will choose the passenger.

I'll go at once!

Amelia was chosen to make the flight. She traveled to Boston to meet the pilot and see the plane.

This is Bill Stultz, the pilot, and Lou Gordan, the mechanic.

And this is the *Friendship!* They're fitting her with pontoons for landing on water.

They had to wait several weeks for the right weather. George Palmer Putnam, one of the men in charge, spent his free time with Amelia.

How did you get into all this, Mr. Putnam?

Oh, I'm a friend of Lindbergh's. I guess I just like to be with people who have adventures!

On June 3, they flew as far as Newfoundland. They had to wait two weeks there. Then on June 17, 1928, they took off for England.

In another twenty-four hours they might be heroes. Or they might be dead.

Shortly after takeoff, they ran into a storm.

Amelia kept a record of what happened.

Bill says the radio is out.

They flew all day and into the night. Were they on the right course?

Sure wish I could check where we are!

We'd better be getting *some-where!*

One of the motors is stalling. I'll dive and try to start it up. Hold on, Amelia!

At 3,000 feet they came out of the fog into dawn light. There was a ship below!

I'll tie a note to an orange and try to hit the ship! I'll ask them to point toward the nearest land!

She tried twice, using the last two oranges. Both missed!

We should see land by now. We have enough gas left for only one hour. Do we land near the ship—or go on?

They went on. Soon they saw small boats below.

Fishing boats! The coast must be near . . . but which way?

And then there it was—land ahead!

Is it England or Ireland?

Who cares? All I want is some calm water to land on!

Bill made a good landing. Lou tied up the plane to keep it from floating away. Amelia waved to a man on shore.

We've crossed two thousand miles of ocean—in twenty hours and forty minutes!

Where is everybody?

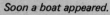

Soon a boat appeared.

We've just flown over from America. Where are we?

Welcome to Burry Port, Wales!

Soon they were welcomed on shore.

There's a great crowd of people waiting to see you, Miss.

Not me—I didn't do anything! It's Bill and Lou who did the flying.

The news flashed around the world. For two weeks they were honored in England. Then they went home to a parade in New York City.

There's Lady Lindy!

Hurray for the first Lady of the Air!

Three cheers for Amelia!

Everywhere it was the same. It was Amelia, the first woman to fly across the Atlantic, who was cheered by the crowds.

But Amelia was unhappy. She talked with George Putnam who was now her friend and manager.

I have to fly the Atlantic by myself!

You *will* do it, I know!

But for now, you must write a book about the *Friendship* flight. We'll call it *Twenty Hours, Forty Minutes.*

Amelia finished the book in a few weeks. Then she returned to flying.

She had bought a small plane in England. She planned to fly across the United States in it.

I'll do it in short hops. I'll stop at night to sleep and to get fuel.

It will be the first time a woman has flown across the country and back again!

From the air, one small town looked like another to Amelia. There were no signs and few airports. One night when her gas was running low, she landed on the main street of Hobbs, New Mexico.

But she reached California and flew home again with no big problems.

Amelia flew in the first Woman's Air Show, wrote stories about flying, and gave many speeches. In 1931, she married George Putnam.

It was an unusual marriage.

I must be free to do my work and to fly. And you must promise to let me go in a year if we are not happy.

I promise!

Amelia kept working to improve her flying. She never forgot her desire to fly across the Atlantic alone. At last, about 7:00 PM on May 20, 1932, she took off from Newfoundland in her airplane.

She climbed to 10,000 feet. The weather was good.

Then something went wrong.

The altimeter is out! I can't tell how high I am!

All at once the plane was in heavy storm clouds.

I'll try to climb above the clouds. But if I go too high, the plane will ice up!

Soon, ice began forming on the wings. The plane went into a spin.

It fell 3,000 feet. The ice melted in the warmer air, and Amelia pulled out of the spin.

That water was too close for comfort!

Suddenly, flames shot out of a crack in the plane's tailpipes. She flew on, hoping it would hold together. Dawn came. She saw land ahead. There were mountains and a railroad.

Perhaps the railroad will lead me to a city with an airport.

Instead, she found a meadow where she made a smooth landing. She had flown from America to Londonderry, Ireland, in fifteen hours, eighteen minutes.

Hello! I've come from America!

Have you, now?

At last she had flown a plane across the Atlantic, alone . . . the first woman to do it!

Lost
Over the
Pacific

In London, the king sent his praise, and she danced with the Prince of Wales.

In Paris they gave her a medal.

The Cross of the Legion of Honor.

The king of Belgium gave her another medal.

Allow my country to honor you.

Back in America she was called to the White House. And President Hoover gave her still another medal.

You are a true American pioneer!

Thank you, Mr. President. I am honored!

Then Amelia flew over the Pacific Ocean from Hawaii to California, the first person, man or woman, to make the flight. Finally, she landed in Newark, New Jersey.

At the airport she and her plane were cheered wildly by the crowds.

NR-965 Y

In 1935, Amelia went to teach at a college in Indiana. She often talked with the women students.

If there is a job you want to try—do it! Don't let being a woman stop you from trying any job!

The college raised money for a special Amelia Earhart Fund.

We have $50,000 to buy you a new airplane!

The Electra was the largest, safest plane she had ever owned. She talked to George about her new plan.

I want to fly around the world in it—at the equator. That's the route no one has flown before.

If that's what you want, I'll do all I can to help you.

While Amelia studied flight charts, George arranged to have gasoline and spare parts at the faraway places where she would need them.

In March, she and Fred Noonan, her navigator, flew to Hawaii. On her next takeoff, something went wrong. There was a crash.

Are you all right?

Yes, and I'll try again!

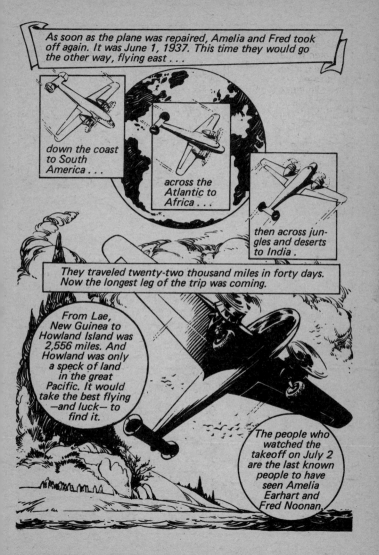

As soon as the plane was repaired, Amelia and Fred took off again. It was June 1, 1937. This time they would go the other way, flying east . . .

down the coast to South America . . .

across the Atlantic to Africa . . .

then across jungles and deserts to India .

They traveled twenty-two thousand miles in forty days. Now the longest leg of the trip was coming.

From Lae, New Guinea to Howland Island was 2,556 miles. And Howland was only a speck of land in the great Pacific. It would take the best flying —and luck— to find it.

The people who watched the takeoff on July 2 are the last known people to have seen Amelia Earhart and Fred Noonan.

The Coast Guard boat Itaska was supposed to help guide Amelia. All night it signaled to her.

Itaska from Earhart . . . we're about 100 miles out . . . please take a bearing on us and report . . .

Earhart from *Itaska* . . . we are sending signals . . . please come in . . .

But Amelia's radio was not receiving the Itaska's signals. Daylight came, and then there was a final message.

Cannot see you. Gas is running low. Can't reach you by radio . . .

At ten o'clock, when her plane would have run out of gas, the United States Navy started the largest sea search in history.

Five ships and sixty planes searched for Amelia's plane. No trace of the Electra or its passengers was found.

It was hard to believe that Amelia Earhart was dead.

Yet how she died is not important. The thirty-nine years of Amelia Earhart's life proved how much one woman could do.

THE END

Do you remember?

Amelia entered college to study:

a. nursing.　　b. medicine.　　c. teaching.

To pay for her flying lessons, Amelia had to get up early and get to her job with:

a. the telephone company.　　　　　　b. the railroad.

c. the pizza shop.

Because she was the first woman to fly across the Atlantic, the crowds cheered Amelia as:

a. Miss Friendship. b. Wonder Woman.

c. Lady Lindy.

When she was seen for the last time, Amelia was:

a. trying to fly around the world.
b. flying from coast to coast.
c. flying to the moon.

Quiz
Yourself

(Answers at end of section)

Words to know

wounded	hurt, injured
altitude	height or distance above the ground
mechanic	someone who fixes motors and engines
unusual	new or different
course	route, planned direction

Can you use them?

Using the words above, complete the following sentences.

1. Today it is not _____ for a woman to be a pilot.

2. "We will be flying at an _____ of 29,000 feet," the pilot said to his passengers.

3. During a war, many people are killed, but many more are _____ .

4. A hundred years ago, a navigator set his _____ by watching the stars; today he uses maps and instruments.

5. To make sure that your car is running correctly, you should have it checked by a _____ every few months.

Using pictures

In reading illustrated stories, you will find it helpful to "read" the pictures as well as the words. Look at this picture of Amelia Earhart outside an army hospital in Canada. Because of her experiences as a nurses' aide, Amelia would always be strongly against war. Now look at pages 40 and 42. Can you find some other things Amelia felt strongly about?

While you are reading

Amelia Earhart received a great deal of attention during her life. But she never let her fame allow her to forget that many people were not as lucky as she was. How many examples can you find to show that Amelia was always thinking of others? While you are reading, list your answers below.

_____

_____

_____

_____

How well did you read?

When you have finished reading, answer the following questions.

1. Which of the following things show that even as a child Amelia was a pioneer?

   (Check the correct *answers.*)

   _____ a. She visited the Indians with her grandmother.

   _____ b. She built her own roller coaster.

   _____ c. She wore bloomers when very few girls had done so.

   _____ d. She took a ride in one of the first flying machines.

2. When did Amelia first know that she wanted to learn to fly?

   (Check the correct answer.)

   _____ a. when her father took her to see an airplane at the Iowa State Fair

   _____ b. when she visited her grandparents in Kansas

   _____ c. after flying across the Atlantic as a passenger in the *Friendship*

   _____ d. when Frank Hawks took her for a ride in his plane

POCKET BIOGRAPHIES

3. What was so special about Amelia's marriage to George Putnam?

   (Check the correct answer.)

   _____ a. George often gave Amelia flying lessons.

   _____ b. George refused to get a job.

   _____ c. George allowed Amelia the freedom to fly and do her work.

   _____ d. Together George and Amelia set many flying records.

4. Why did Amelia want to fly across the Atlantic Ocean alone?

   (Check the correct answer.)

   _____ a. She hoped to win the prize money that was being offered for the flight.

   _____ b. She wanted to prove that being a woman shouldn't stop a person from doing something.

   _____ c. She wanted to test a new airplane.

   _____ d. She hoped the trip would help sell her book.

5. Which of the following problems did Amelia have on her record solo flight across the Atlantic?

   (Check the correct *answers*.)

   _____ a. The altimeter did not work.

   _____ b. She flew in the wrong direction.

   _____ c. The plane ran low on gas.

   _____ d. Ice formed on the wings of the plane.

   _____ e. Flames shot out of the plane's tailpipe.

Using what you've read

When the *Electra* was lost on its flight around the world, no one could believe that Amelia Earhart was dead. Even today, people keep her memory alive by remembering the records she set and by admiring her courage. Write a brief summary of the things Amelia did which give her a lasting place in American history. Include Amelia's special qualities which you believe will help people remember her for years to come.

ANSWER KEY

AMELIA EARHART

Can you use them?

1. unusual
2. altitude
3. wounded
4. course
5. mechanic

How well did you read?

1. b, c
2. d
3. c
4. b
5. a, d, e

NOTES

NOTES

NOTES

NOTES

COMPLETE LIST OF POCKET CLASSICS AVAILABLE

CLASSICS

COMPLETE LIST OF POCKET CLASSICS AVAILABLE
(cont'd)

COMPLETE LIST OF POCKET CLASSICS AVAILABLE
(cont'd)

SHAKESPEARE

BIOGRAPHIES

B 1 Charles Lindbergh
B 2 Amelia Earhart
B 3 Houdini
B 4 Walt Disney
B 5 Davy Crockett
B 6 Daniel Boone
B 7 Elvis Presley
B 8 The Beatles
B 9 Benjamin Franklin
B10 Martin Luther King, Jr.
B11 Abraham Lincoln
B12 Franklin D. Roosevelt
B13 George Washington
B14 Thomas Jefferson
B15 Madame Curie
B16 Albert Einstein
B17 Thomas Edison
B18 Alexander Graham Bell
B19 Vince Lombardi
B20 Pelé
B21 Babe Ruth
B22 Jackie Robinson
B23 Jim Thorpe
B24 Althea Gibson